101
Things a College Guy Should Know

I've written this little book because I'm convinced that sometimes a few choice words can make a bigger difference than anything you'll find in a five hundred-page guidebook. The advice here comes from the real world. It's based on some things I did wrong, some things my friends did wrong, and some things all first-year students (and some fifth-year students) do wrong. I hope you can learn from our experiences. Good luck!

Stephen Edwards

1

Although it's tempting to slack, get a summer job before you go away to school.

Parents never give you enough money.

2

Take many pairs of underwear with you.

You can put off all other laundry for weeks.

3

Get a laundry bag and basket and use them!

4

Take the time to read, and follow, the instructions on the back of the detergent box.

5

Get a durable backpack and put your name in it.

It should last all four years.

6

Put some thought into packing your clothes to bring to school.

You need more than baseball hats and T-shirts.

7

Don't forget to bring a coat and tie.

8

Bring pictures of friends for your dorm room.

Dorms can be cold and impersonal.

9

Buy a school sweatshirt.

You'll wear it the rest of your life.

10

Bring a box of extra essentials (deodorant, toothpaste, shaving cream, razors).

11

Buy fifteen pairs of matching socks.

You'll wear them every day and won't have to worry about those socks lost in the dryer.

12

Know that you can never have too many towels.

13

Get stamps (a huge supply) before you leave home.

14

Save the boxes you shipped your stuff to school in.

Most dorms have storage space.

15
Begin budgeting yourself the minute you arrive.

16
Try to meet as many people on your dorm floor as possible.

You'll stay friends with them for the next four years.

17

At winter break, take and leave at home any clothes you haven't worn since September.

18

Whenever a professor offers office hours, visit him/her.

It can raise a borderline grade.

19

If possible, have all your papers read by student tutors.

20

Learn the library IMMEDIATELY!!!

21

Write ALL assignments down.

If not, you'll always forget one.

22

Read what is assigned.

It saves you from impossible cramming at exam time.

23

Read what is assigned.

Even if the professor doesn't call on students.

24

Read ahead!

25

Get a date book and record all long-term projects on syllabus day.

26

Try to schedule your classes early in the morning or all in the afternoon.

27

Don't start the weekend on Thursday.

28

Don't go out on any weeknight when you have a class before 9:30 the next morning.

29

Learn to use all the word process-
ing and spreadsheet programs
while they are easily accessible.

30
Sit in the front of the classroom.
Professors notice.

31
Talk in class.
But remember to listen too.

32

Don't cheat yourself by using *Cliffs Notes*.

You'll wish you had read the whole book later.

33

Never turn in someone's old papers.

You'd be surprised at what professors remember.

34

Proofread all your papers, then have someone else proofread them.

35

Always have a good dictionary and thesaurus handy.

36

After two years at school, visit the Career Counseling office.

37

Make sure your adviser knows your goals, interests, and weaknesses.

If not get a new one.

38

Know that registering for classes is HELL.

39

Never forge your adviser's signature on registration documents.

Advisers know about prerequisites and core classes that you may not.

40

Be prepared to change your major twenty-seven times.

41

Read a nonassigned novel every month.

42

Read at least the front-page stories of a newspaper every day.

There are papers from all over the country in the library.

43

Read your school paper cover to cover.

44

If your parents are looking
for a way to help, ask for rolls
of quarters.

They are like gold on campus.

45

If possible, take extra fruit from the cafeteria for late-night snacking. *AVOID THE VENDING MACHINES.*

46

Don't buy notebooks in the university bookstore. ($$$.)

47

Don't get drunk and order pizza.

It costs a lot and you'll get a gut.

48

Don't miss on-campus meals.

Ordering out will bankrupt you.

49

Heartily greet and thank the cafeteria workers.

They'll remember you and slip you extras.

50

Write as few checks as possible.

Your ATM card will work till you have to pay rent and bills.

51

Don't withdraw more cash than you can afford to spend.

If you have it, you'll spend it.

52

Learn to balance a checkbook.

The more accurate you are, the more likely the chance that your parents will give you a loan.

53
DON'T BOUNCE CHECKS.

54
Don't apply for credit cards until your junior year.

55

If offered any type of on-campus job, take it.

The hours are good, and you can usually take time off to study.

56

Save money to buy a computer.

Many places offer student rates.

57

Buy a used bike with an unbreakable lock.

Graduating seniors always sell bikes—check the bulletin boards.

58

Never underestimate the importance of water.

Too much beer = dehydration.

59

Always go to the health service and get a doctor's excuse for missed classes, even when faking.

60

Hold office in the student government, a fraternity, or a club.

61

Join whatever clubs or campus organizations you have time for.

62

Write for the school paper or literary magazine.

63

Take one of the free courses offered (karate, tennis, etc.) at the school gym/recreation center.

These classes will cost a lot more after you graduate.

64

Play on an intramural sports team.

65

Learn to fall asleep with the lights on.

You and your roommate will never go to bed at the same time.

66

Learn to negotiate and work out conflicts with roommates.

67

Always lock your dorm room.

Your next-door neighbor could be a recovering klepto.

68

Keep a box of microwave popcorn stashed away for emergencies.

69

Have friends of many different races, orientations, and religions.

70

With a roommate, remember your mess is shared with another.

71

Work out a bathroom cleaning schedule.

Once a semester is not enough.

72

Don't borrow anything without asking.

73

Return what you borrow in the same condition.

74

Find a friend with a car.

But don't abuse the favor.

75

Never, ever leave your wash unattended.

Some people will steal anything.

76

Listen to college radio.

It's a great way to hear cutting-edge music that's played nowhere else.

77

Study at quirky coffee shops that play interesting music.

78

Do something outdoors on Sunday mornings.

79

Tutor challenged kids after school.

80

Volunteer with a local charity.

81

Wait awhile to move off campus.

The temptation to blow off school will be too great.

82

No matter how tired you are,
always brush your teeth before
bed.

83

Remember: Women you meet Saturday at 2:00 A.M. you'll probably have class with Monday at 9:00 A.M.

84

Don't get a bad reputation.

They are easy to gain and hard to lose—
for guys as well as girls.

85

Always be protected.

86

Attend a "Take Back the Night" rally with a female friend.

87

Think of every girl as somebody's sister.

88
Know that everyone gets homesick.

89
Write or e-mail—don't call—friends from home.

A return letter is much better than a phone call. And it's cheaper, too.

90

Remember your grandparents on their birthdays.

They will always remember you.

91

If invited to dinner at a local student's home, never refuse.

Home cooking and a family atmosphere make a great cure for homesickness.

92

Make a friend you can really talk to.

93

Don't let the frenzy of rush cloud your judgment.

Choose a fraternity that meets your needs and suits your style.

94

Don't tolerate cruel and unusual hazing.

95

Don't let your girlfriend sleep
at your frat house.

96

Don't even try to spend the night
at a sorority house.

97

Remember that everyone was a freshman once.

98

Be confident and happy with who you are.

It shows!

99

Don't worry about having a serious girlfriend your freshman year.

100

Know that high school, long-distance relationships rarely last through second semester freshman year.

101

Allow yourself to grow, change, err, love, ache, party, learn, and search in order to become the man you are meant to be.